A HISTORY OF
ASHTON VILLA

Library of Congress Cataloging-in-Publication Data

Hafertepe, Kenneth, 1955–
    A history of Ashton Villa: a family and its house in Victorian Galveston, Texas /
Kenneth Hafertepe.
        p.   cm.   — (Popular history series ; no. 5)
    Includes bibliographical references.
    ISBN 0-87611-112-6 (paper : acid-free): $5.95
    1. Ashton Villa (Galveston, Tex.) 2. Ashton Villa (Museum) 3. Brown Family.
4. Galveston (Tex.)—Social life and customs. 5. Galveston (Tex.)—Biography.
6. Galveston (Tex.)—Buildings, structures, etc. 7. Architecture, Domestic—
Texas—Galveston.
I. Title. II. Series.
F394.G2H18   1991
976.4'139—dc20   91-13918
                                                                                                            CIP

Number five in the Popular History Series
ISBN: 0-87611-112-6
Design by David Timmons

Published by the Texas State Historical Association in cooperation with the
Center for Studies in Texas History at the University of Texas at Austin.

Cover: Ashton Villa, 1991, photograph © Jim Cruz. All Rights Reserved.

A HISTORY OF
ASHTON VILLA

*A Family and Its House in
Victorian Galveston, Texas*

KENNETH HAFERTEPE

TEXAS STATE
HISTORICAL ASSOCIATION

CONTENTS

INTRODUCTION

New Year's Day

ONE OF THE MOST FESTIVE OCCASIONS of the year in Galveston, Texas, in the Victorian era was New Year's Day. It was a day for sharing hospitality with friends and neighbors, for dining and drinking and dancing to toast in the new year. Few houses in Galveston have played host to as many New Year's Day celebrations as the home of Mr. and Mrs. James Moreau Brown, known as Ashton Villa.

During the day the house was open to callers, who would be courteously received by James and Rebecca Brown, by their children, particularly the beautiful and talented Miss Bettie, and, in later years, by numerous grandchildren. The night brought a magnificent ball. Horse-drawn carriages clattered down Broadway and deposited their riders in front of the stately Italianate mansion, which glowed from the light of gas chandeliers. Ladies in long gowns and gentlemen in their most formal attire walked on a red carpet past the ornate corn-stalk gateposts, along the brick walk, up the steps and into the house. The tall ceilings of the first floor rooms would echo with music and laughter.

Begun in 1859, and completed as the clouds of war were gathering in the East, Ashton Villa was a house of many uses. It was built for intimate and even tender domestic scenes, for grand social occasions, and to announce that its owner was one of the wealthiest citizens of Galveston. It also announced that its owner was a man of taste who was familiar with the latest East Coast architectural fashions. Ashton Villa was one of the first Texas residences in the Italianate style, adapted from a design in *The Model Architect* by the Philadelphia architect Samuel Sloan. It is now the oldest surviving mansion on Broadway, a boulevard long recognized as a locus of power and wealth in Galveston.

Ashton Villa is also a sturdy survivor of natural and man-made hazards. Its brick walls have weathered many a storm, including the Great Hurricane of 1900, when floodwaters invaded its first floor. Subsequently it served for many years as the headquarters of a fraternal organization. Facing the possibility of demolition in the 1960s, it was purchased in 1970 by the Galveston Historical Foundation, a critical turning point in the historic preservation movement in Galveston. Now, as a historic house museum, it is well cared for and well attended. Ashton Villa, filled with furniture and memorabilia dating to the residence of the Brown family, speaks eloquently about the lives and aspirations of an upper-class Texas family in the nineteenth and early twentieth centuries.

1.
FROM NEW YORK
TO GALVESTON

JAMES MOREAU BROWN was born in New York State on September 22, 1821. His parents, John M. and Hannah Krantz Brown, were of Dutch descent, and had sixteen children, of whom James Moreau Brown was the last. Young James seems to have been full of restless energy: according to one biographical account, he ran away from home at age twelve and was gone for two years. This account further claims that after another year at home he ran away to work on the Erie Canal, then returned home to be apprenticed to a brick mason. Another account says that he was apprenticed at age twelve to learn the brick mason's and plasterer's trades and that he remained an apprentice until age sixteen. Around 1838 he left New York, sailing to Charleston, South Carolina. He worked his way across the South, building courthouses, jails, and cisterns. He stayed briefly in New Orleans before settling for several years in Vicksburg, Mississippi.[1]

In the mid-1840s James M. Brown moved to the recently founded island city of Galveston, Texas. Galveston Island divides Galveston Bay from the Gulf of Mexico, and the landward side of the island is thus an excellent natural harbor, capable of receiving inland trade which came down the Trinity River into the bay and providing ample wharfage for seagoing vessels.[2]

The city of Galveston was founded in 1836 and originally occupied only the eastern tip of the island. The city plan was a neat rectilinear grid, more or less oriented to the points of the compass but precisely parallel to the shoreline of the harbor. The second street south of the harbor, known as The Strand, became the commercial

Plan of the City of Galveston, Texas by William H. Sandusky, 1845. Courtesy Rosenberg Library, Galveston.

center of Galveston and, indeed, of Texas. When Brown came to Texas, the city proper was between The Strand and Broadway; between Broadway and the Gulf were vacant lots and the suburban estates of the founders of Galveston, such as Michael Menard, Samuel May Williams, and Gail Borden, Jr.

In 1847 Brown entered the hardware business in partnership with Henry H. Brower under the name of Brown and Brower. Together they purchased from John S. Sydnor and Alfred T. James a lot on the south side of Market Street, between 26th and 25th streets, on which they built their store. Also included among the assets of the firm were three slaves: Austin, a thirty-four-year-old man; Sophia, a woman; and her daughter, Harriet, who presumably had been owned by Brower. Brown already owned a slave named Lucy and her three children, John, Francis, and Henry, but he sold Lucy and her children for $850 to Eliza J. Bourman of Harris County in May of 1847. In June of 1848 Brown bought out Brower's interest in the firm, worth some $1,450, including the buildings and property on Market Street, all stock and materials on hand, and all three slaves. Austin was in Brown's service for less than ten years, but Sophia and Harriet were to become longtime servants of the Brown family.[3]

Galveston by G. Hooten, 1839. Oil on canvas, 25 x 40 inches. *Courtesy Rosenberg Library, Galveston.*

Brown's fortunes were steadily rising. In 1848 he was elected to serve as an alderman on the Galveston City Council. At the time he was still in his mid-twenties, an indication that his fellow Galvestonians esteemed this young man as someone devoted to the growth of his adopted city. Brown would serve two more terms on the city council, in 1871 and 1872, when the city was struggling to recover from the effects of the Civil War.[4]

Brown was advancing rapidly in the realms of business and public affairs, but as yet he had no one to share with him his triumphs and adversities. In the mid-1840s a young lady moved to the island who would soon win his heart, Rebecca Ashton Stoddart Rhodes. Rebecca was born in Philadelphia on November 18, 1831, the daughter of John Ashton Stoddart and his wife Sarah. John Stoddart was descended from a Revolutionary War veteran, Lieutenant Isaac Ashton, and worked as an agent for the New York Coal Company. According to family tradition, John Stoddart died when his daughter Rebecca was quite young, and Sarah Stoddart later married C. K. Rhodes, a New Jersey native and an auctioneer. The family moved to Galveston in 1845 or 1846 and settled in a little wooden house at Avenue I and 19th Street. The family attended Trinity Episcopal Church, and there Rebecca met James M. Brown.[5]

James and Rebecca were married in the original wood-framed Gothic-style Trinity Church on April 9, 1848. The service was performed by the Reverend Mr. Benjamin Eaton, who had been the rector of Trinity since its establishment in 1841. At the time of their marriage, James was twenty-six, and Rebecca sixteen. Before the year was out she presented James M. Brown with a son, John Stoddart Brown, born on December 9, 1848.[6]

With a wife and a child to support, Brown set about improving his property on Market Street. He erected "a two-story dwelling house built of and covered with wood," which had a completely separate kitchen building in the rear of the house. At first the two-story frame building served both as his hardware store and his home, but after 1850 it was used exclusively as a residence. After the Browns built Ashton Villa, they sold their house on Market Street for $3,500 in 1861.[7]

Brown took on a new partner in the hardware business in 1850. This was Stephen Kirkland, like Brown a native of New York. Kirkland

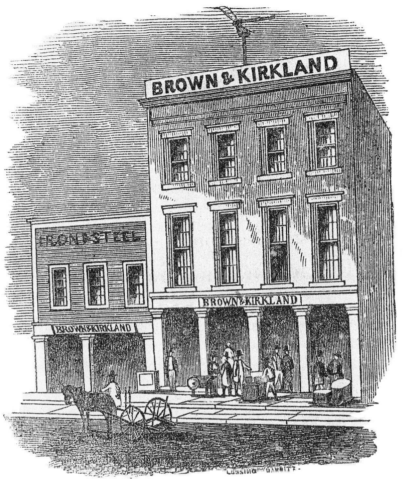

Brown and Kirkland Hardware Store, Galveston. From the *Texas Almanac for 1857.*
Courtesy the Barker Texas History Center, The University of Texas at Austin.

was seven years Brown's senior and had been in Galveston since 1838. He served as an alderman in 1841 and again in 1847 and 1853. In 1850 Kirkland married Mary A. Emerson, a native of Maine who had come to live in Galveston with her father, Joseph Emerson, after the death of her mother Rebecca. Stephen and Mary Kirkland were close friends of James and Rebecca Brown, and many decades later one of the Brown daughters, Mathilda, would write in her diary of visiting "Auntie" Kirkland.[8]

Brown & Kirkland was situated on The Strand, the great commercial street of Galveston and, indeed, of nineteenth-century Texas. The company sold all kinds of foreign and domestic hardware, including "agricultural implements, iron & steel, nails, . . . paints, oils and window glass, and every article appertaining to the general hardware business. " In 1855 the partners signed a complex agreement with Theodore and Gustavus Oppermann by which Brown & Kirkland would erect a new building for the hardware store on a lot on The Strand which the Oppermanns owned. Brown & Kirkland would design the building, furnish some of the materials—probably all of the hardware—and supervise its construction. The firm would then lease it for five years.[9]

The Brown & Kirkland Hardware Store was to be a "three story brick house," with a frontage of nearly 30 feet and a depth of 100 feet, and not to cost more than $10,000. The building was in the Greek Revival style, with five square Doric piers defining the first floor and simple, unadorned lintels and sills on the two floors above. Although this building has been demolished, an old woodcut shows it to have been quite similar to the Hendley Building, one block east on The Strand, also begun in 1855 but not finished until 1859. Both buildings were strongly indebted to the Pontalba buildings on Jackson Square in New Orleans, built to the designs of James Gallier and Henry Howard and completed in 1851. James M. Brown seems to have been very much aware of recent architectural trends, a trait which would again become evident when he built a new home.[10]

Late in 1855 Brown purchased another slave, this one from Daniel D. Atchison, a lawyer. The slave's name was Aleck, and he was described in the contract as "aged about 30 years, of dark color, about 5 feet 10 inches, and by trade a brick mason." Aleck was a high-priced slave, costing $1,500, an indication that he was a highly skilled craftsman. It is especially significant that Aleck was trained as a mason, given that Brown was engaged in the erection of a new hardware store. Brown may have purchased Aleck to work on his store and also may have been thinking that he might one day build a grand brick residence, which no one in Galveston had yet done.[11]

In addition to the hardware business, Brown also branched out into the sale and repair of buggies. This was known as J. M. Brown's Carriage Repository, which was located next to Brown & Kirkland on The Strand. There "carriages, buggies, and every description of vehicles" could be purchased, or older models could be "painted and trimmed in a neat and fashionable style. " His partner in this enterprise was Joseph Stowe, a Massachusetts native who had served with Andrew Jackson during the War of 1812. Stowe was an "old, established, and well known carriage maker," having resided in Galveston since 1844. The partnership with Brown, however, lasted only for a few years.[12]

The family of James and Rebecca Brown continued to grow. A second son, Moreau Roberts Brown, was born July 26, 1853. Little more than a year and a half later, Rebecca Ashton Brown was born on February 18, 1855. Named after her mother, she would be known as Bettie. The Browns were to have two more children in the early 1860s, but by then the family would be living in a grand new home.[13]

The year 1859 was a watershed in the life of James and Rebecca Brown. In May of that year Brown's business partner, Stephen Kirkland, died at age forty-four. Brown then accepted the position of president of the Galveston, Houston & Henderson Railroad, which had completed nearly forty miles of track. Brown oversaw the completion of the bridge, which connected the island with the mainland, and the completion of the line into Houston. Another important event of 1859 occurred on January 6, when Brown paid $4,000 for lots 11 to 14 on block 203, the north side of Broadway between 23rd and 24th. On this land Brown would build a house, which stands today and for which he is best remembered: Ashton Villa.[14]

2.
BUILDING
ASHTON VILLA

BY THE END OF THE 1850s, Galveston was a bustling city of more than 7,000 people. Its residents could boast of two brick churches—St. Mary's Catholic and Trinity Episcopal—and numerous multistory brick buildings on The Strand: the Hendley Building, the Brown & Kirkland Building, the J. C. Kuhn Building, and the R. & D. G. Mills Building. A new brick federal customhouse was in the planning stages. In addition, there were several buildings with cast-iron fronts, which had been shipped from New York and Philadelphia, including the stores of E. S. Wood and Henry Rosenberg. At the beginning of 1859, however, Galveston was predominantly a city of wooden houses. James M. Brown resolved to build a brick house that would also be the most stylish, up-to-date in Galveston.[1]

For the design of his house Brown turned to a recent book by the Philadelphia architect Samuel Sloan, *The Model Architect*. Sloan was a native of Chester, Pennsylvania, who came to architecture through carpentry and the building trades. *The Model Architect* was published in 1852, when Sloan's career was just taking off and nearly a decade before his most famous commission, Dr. Haller Nutt's octagonal house in Natchez, Mississippi: Longwood. *The Model Architect* featured plans, elevations, details, and even specifications for houses in a variety of styles: Italian, Gothic, Elizabethan, Norman, even Oriental. In his eclecticism Sloan was following the lead of Andrew Jackson Downing, who had illustrated similar houses in his books *Cottage Residences* (1842) and *The Architecture of Country Houses* (1850).[2]

The house which caught James M. Brown's eye was Design XXI, entitled "A Suburban Residence" and described by Sloan as "a three-

"A Suburban Residence" from Samuel Sloan's *The Model Architect* (Philadelphia, 1851), Plate LXXXVII. *Courtesy Athenaeum of Philadelphia.*

storied country mansion," made of brick and with a tin roof. Sloan's house was a great squarish block with a low hipped roof. It had three wide bays, each with paired windows. The central bay broke forward to create a vestibule, and atop this central projection was a small pediment. The eaves projected dramatically all around the house, and nestled under the eaves were brackets, a popular feature on early Victorian houses in the United States.[3]

Instead of three bays of paired windows, Brown used five bays of single windows, which deemphasized the central bay and changed the patterning of the brackets under the eaves. He also limited the use of round-arched windows to those on the third floor and on the front and rear doors. To enhance the appearance of the now flat-arched windows, Brown added cast-iron window moldings derived from Sloan's Design VIII, "An Italian Residence." But the most dramatic departure from Sloan's "Suburban Residence" was in the treatment of the veranda. Sloan's design had two side verandas which wrapped around the back and which were joined by a passage separating the main block of the house from the kitchen wing. Brown eliminated the one-story side verandas and added the two-story, three-bay cast-iron veranda to the main facade.

The cast-iron veranda at Ashton Villa beautifully combines strength and delicacy. The colonnettes rise to form arches that recall both Gothic and Moorish design, and hanging from the second floor are bunches of grapes alternating with acanthus leaves. The cast-iron work is very fine and almost certainly was ordered from the iron foundry of Wood & Perot of Philadelphia. The veranda at Ashton Villa is extremely similar to a Moorish design illustrated in the Wood & Perot catalogue. James M. Brown could have seen an advertisement for the Wood & Perot foundry which ran in the *Civilian and Galveston Gazette* in the summer of 1858, offering "iron railings for cemeteries, public buildings, and verandas. " In fact, the local agent for Wood & Perot, E. S. Wood, had already erected a building at 23rd and Mechanic with a cast-iron front from Sanson and Farrand, another Philadelphia foundry. It is certain that the cast-iron fence that

The J. M. Brown Residence, Ashton Villa. Photograph from the 1860s. *Courtesy Rosenberg Library, Galveston.* The original two-story outbuilding for the kitchen is visible at the right.

Detail from *A Bird's Eye View of the City of Galveston, Texas* drawn by C. Drie, 1871. *Courtesy Rosenberg Library, Galveston.* "A" marks Ashton Villa, "B" marks the previous J. M. Brown House on Market Street. This view shows the rear of Ashton Villa, so that the stable block, the kitchen, and the connecting arcade are clearly visible.

enclosed the house was imported from Philadelphia, because one of the gateposts is marked "Wood & Perot, Phil*a.* " These gateposts have delightful corn-stalk finials, which were also used on houses in the French Quarter and in the Garden District of New Orleans.[4]

The brick used at Ashton Villa may have been made by Brown himself, by a local manufacturer, or imported from elsewhere in the United States. Brown did not engage in the commercial manufacture of brick, but as a trained brick mason he probably was capable of

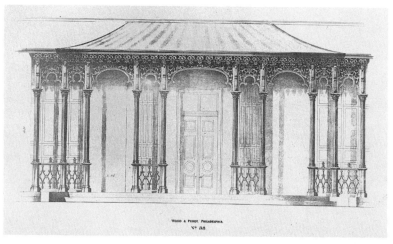

No. 201.
WOOD & PEROT, Philadelphia,

Above: Design for a veranda from *Wood and Perot's Portfolio of Original Designs of . . . Ornamental Ironwork* (1858), Design No. 38. *Courtesy Henry Francis du Pont Winterthur Museum.*

Below: Corn-stalk gate post from *Wood and Perot's Portfolio of Original Designs of . . . Ornamental Ironwork* (1858), Design No. 201. *Courtesy Henry Francis du Pont Winterthur Museum.*

Corn-stalk gate post, Ashton Villa. *Courtesy Galveston Historical Foundation.*

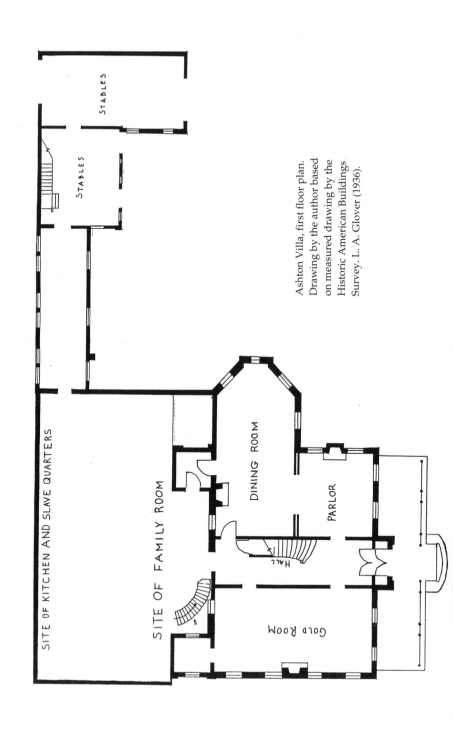

Ashton Villa, first floor plan. Drawing by the author based on measured drawing by the Historic American Buildings Survey. L. A. Glover (1936).

making the brick for his own house. Other sources were available, however. In the 1850s Dr. Nicholas Labadie offered for sale bricks made in Galveston, and bricks made on White Oak Bayou near Houston were also available. Texas-made bricks cost around ten dollars per thousand, but brick from Mobile, Pensacola, or even Baltimore could be shipped in for fourteen dollars per thousand. Whatever the source of the brick, it is certain that they were laid with great precision by Brown's highly trained slave, Aleck.[5]

The floor plan of Ashton Villa was essentially a reversed version of Sloan's "Suburban Residence. " In Sloan's plan a vestibule led into the central hall, which had its staircase on the left side; to the right of the hall was a double parlor, to the left an office and a dining room. At Ashton Villa the vestibule was much smaller, and the stairway was on the right side of the hall. A large parlor (what is now the Gold Room) was to the left, a small parlor and the dining room to the right. The kitchen was in a separate building behind the main house. Brown increased the dimensions of all the first-floor rooms, another indication that he was looking for a monumental effect.[6]

The interior of the villa had two principal ornamental features. One was the use of a simple, heavy frame for doors and windows throughout the house. These door and window frames were very similar to a door frame illustrated as part of Sloan's Design I, "An Italian Villa. " These frames were not radically different from frames used in Greek Revival houses—indeed, the doorway leading from the sitting room to the dining room is a shouldered architrave, a Greek form popularized by Minard Lafever in *The Beauties of Modern Architecture* (1835) and used extensively by Abner Cook in the Governor's Mansion and other Greek Revival houses in Austin. Sloan included only one design that featured shouldered architraves on the exterior: Design XXXVI, "The Parsonage. " The other principal ornamental feature was the cornice. In each room on the first floor the point where the wall met the ceiling was marked by a plaster border in a curving floral pattern. Similar floral patterns could be found in Sloan's Design XVII, "Italian Houses."

Ashton Villa had all of the modern conveniences available in 1859. There was a built-in closet for each bedroom, taking the place of a free-standing wardrobe. Each of the front bedrooms had a small room with a sink, and the rear bedrooms had full bathrooms, which received water from cisterns in the attic. Another underground cistern supplied water to the kitchen. The house also had its own gas heating and lighting system, one of the first in Texas. One of the original gas chandeliers, called "gasoliers," is visible in photographs of the Gold Room taken in the 1890s. There was also a gas heating system in the basement, but Brown also installed coal fireplaces.[7]

Two brick outbuildings, two stories each and connected by a brick arcade, ran along the northern property line of the house. The kitchen was immediately behind the main house, separated from it by a narrow courtyard. The lower floor contained the kitchen and a laundry room, and the upper floor was slave quarters for Aleck, Harriet, and Sophia. The stable occupied the northeast corner of the property. J. M. Brown did not own a great many horses: he bought one in 1859, and a second in 1862, and a carriage soon thereafter.

None of the furniture bought in 1859 is still in the house, and evidence is sketchy as to how the Browns had it furnished. When J. M. Brown died in 1895, his obituary claimed that "some of the parlor furniture is the same that he selected in New York after completing his new home." Given that the manufacture of furniture in Texas was in its infancy, it would not be surprising if a first-rate home was furnished with pieces from the East Coast or even Europe.[8]

Historic photographs of the Gold Room taken in the 1890s show that the Browns owned a sofa, a pair of armchairs and a pair of side chairs in the French Antique style, which was extremely popular between 1840 and 1860. Originally these chairs would have been unpainted, but around 1890 they were painted white and gilded. In 1850 Andrew Jackson Downing praised French furniture in *The Architecture of Country Houses*, noting that "its union of lightness, elegance, and grace renders it especially the favorite of ladies. For country houses we would confine its use, chiefly, to the drawing-room or boudoir, using the more simple and massive classical forms for the library, dining-room and other apartments. " Indeed, the Browns' settee, with its curving back and delicate carving, is extremely similar to Downing's Figure 238, "a drawing-room sofa in the Louis Quatorze style."[9]

The Browns did not have to travel to New York for such furniture; it could be purchased in Galveston at the "House-Furnishing

Warerooms" of J. M. Sauter on Tremont Street. One writer in 1858 speculated that "a family can arrive at Galveston at nine o'clock in the morning, engage a house, and, by having the funds at their command (for Sauter does nothing but a cash business) they can be snugly settled `at home' before the going down of the sun. " At Sauter's one could purchase "fine English carpets, French china, Bohemian glassware, and Northern furniture, from the magnificent rose-wood piano down to the humble washboard. " Moreover, Sauter was then abroad in Europe, selecting and shipping even more items. It would seem likely that Ashton Villa was furnished from Sauter's as well as from the Browns' own shopping forays to the North.[10]

The name Ashton Villa blends family tradition with contemporary architectural terminology. James and Rebecca used old family names for their children—including Ashton, Moreau, Rhodes, and Stoddart—and Ashton, the name of Rebecca's father, was used for the house as well. "Villa" was a Roman term for a rural retreat or country place, and the term was extremely popular in the 1840s and 1850s, especially for houses in picturesque styles like the Gothic and the Italian. Samuel Sloan commented in 1851 that the Italian villa "has been introduced into other parts of Europe, into England and America, and so well adapted is it to the wants and tastes of our people, that it is likely to become, if it is not already, one of our most fashionable modes of building. " Sloan did not call the design on which the Browns' house was based a villa but a "Suburban Residence," and, indeed, Ashton Villa certainly made an urbane statement in 1859 Galveston.[11]

When Ashton Villa was completed, the Browns had one of the most impressive houses on the island. It was also one of the most expensive houses in Texas. J. M. Brown paid $4,000 just for the land on which his house was to be built, and by the time the house was completed the property was worth $18,000. Very few houses in antebellum Texas cost this much: the Governor's Mansion, built between 1854 and 1856, cost $3,500 for its city block and $14,500 for the house itself. Brown had sought to build one of the most expensive and imposing residences in Texas, and he had succeeded.[12]

Ashton Villa may have been completed as early as New Year's Day of 1860, but it is certain that the house was finished by February of 1861, when J. M. Brown sold their old house on Market Street to

Hugh Prichard for $3,500. The Browns moved just one block east and six blocks south, but they went from an ordinary wood-frame house to one of the finest and most up-to-date in Texas. J. M. Brown and his family were to live in their grand new house for the better part of seventy years.[13]

3.
LIFE AT
THE VILLA

THE BROWNS HAD LITTLE TIME to enjoy their new home before the bombardment of Fort Sumter ushered in the Civil War. Most Galvestonians were strongly in favor of secession—they voted 765 to 33 in favor of leaving the Union—but J. M. Brown was firmly opposed. He did not serve in the Confederate Army, although as president of the Galveston, Houston & Henderson Railroad he assisted Confederate general John B. Magruder in moving troops and supplies between Galveston and Houston. He also served the Confederate government as a purchasing agent in Mexico, trading cotton for supplies. In recognition of his service to the Confederacy, General Magruder bestowed upon Brown the honorary title of colonel, which he proudly used for the rest of his life.[1]

The Brown family continued to grow. Charles Rhodes Brown, named for Rebecca Brown's stepfather, was born in the house on March 21, 1862, and Mathilda Ella Brown, the last of James and Rebecca's children, was born after the war on September 26, 1865. The Browns' eldest son, John Stoddart Brown, hoped to become a college professor, and during the war years he studied at Rugby, England, and at Stuttgart, Germany. He learned to speak the language fluently and specialized in German literature. Twice during his residence in Europe he accompanied the Reverend Benjamin Eaton, the rector of Trinity Church in Galveston, on tours of the Continent. Unfortunately John's studies were curtailed when he caught pneumonia; he returned to Texas in order to fully recuperate.[2]

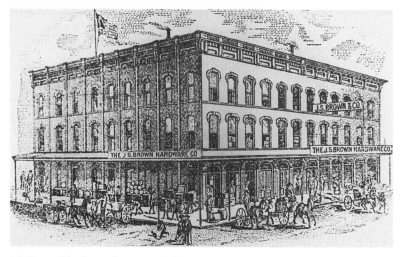

J. S. Brown Hardware Company Building, 2226-2228 Strand. *Courtesy Rosenberg Library, Galveston.*

On June 19, 1865, Union general Gordon Granger landed at Galveston and declared the Emancipation Proclamation effective in Texas. In September 1865 J. M. Brown was the first Galvestonian to travel to Washington to take the oath of allegiance to the United States. His three slaves were free to go, but they continued to work for him. The Brown children grew up knowing the slave who built the brick walls of Ashton Villa as "Uncle Aleck. " In 1871 and 1872 Reconstruction governor E. J. Davis appointed Brown to serve on the Galveston City Council.[3]

After the war James M. Brown re-entered the hardware business, this time in partnership with John Lang, a native of Germany and a longtime Galveston merchant. As with Brown & Kirkland, their hardware store was on The Strand. By 1868 Brown & Lang kept on hand $40,000 in merchandise—ten years earlier Brown & Kirkland had kept $10,000 in merchandise—and this had increased to $70,000 by 1873. When the younger Brown returned from his studies in Europe, he entered the firm of Brown & Lang as a clerk, and over the next ten years he learned the business. In April of 1875 Lang retired from the firm, and J. S. Brown became a full partner, the firm now being known as J. S. Brown & Company.[4]

J. M. Brown had been prosperous before the Civil War, but his wealth multiplied after the war. By the time of the 1870 census Brown owned $175,000 in real estate and $100,000 in personal property (which included investments and cash on hand). This made Brown the third wealthiest man in Galveston, behind his fellow merchants J. J. Hendley and John Sealy but well ahead of other merchant princes such as E. B. Nichols, Robert Mills, and Henry Rosenberg. Indeed, in 1870 Brown was the fifth wealthiest Texan: first was Richard King, cattleman and founder of the legendary King Ranch in South Texas; tied for second were Hendley and Sealy; and fourth was Amanda Cartwright of San Augustine, who listed her occupation as housekeeper but who was also the matriarch of a landed East Texas family. Before the war the wealthiest Texans tended to be planters or farmers, but by 1870 they had been replaced by merchants and bankers.[5]

Not surprisingly, the elder Brown was also involved in the organization of the First National Bank of Galveston. When the bank president, T. H. McMahan, died in 1871, Brown was elected to succeed him. A contemporary account praised Brown as "an able and shrewd financier" who "looks closely after the affairs of this solid bank. " Brown was also personally responsible for seeing that the bank building was solid, for his obituary reported that he superintended the erection of the building. This red brick structure, at the southeast corner of 22nd and The Strand, had columns, an entablature, and a cornice made of cast-iron. Its style was decidedly the commercial version of the Italianate, with elaborate Corinthian columns, arched window hoods, and brackets lining the cornice.[6]

In 1870 John S. Brown married Helen Delespine, and two years later he purchased a house two blocks west of his father's house on Broadway. The house, which he named Live Oak Terrace, was an example of the Greek Revival style. Four two-story Doric columns formed a gallery on both the first and second floors. The front steps were guarded by a pair of cast-iron lions, which were said to have been brought from Europe. The purchase of a house was a sign that John, at age twenty-four, was rising within the firm and acquiring some financial independence.[7]

When James and Rebecca Brown paid their property taxes in 1874, they declared $1,600 worth of household furniture. This was the first

First National Bank of Galveston, Twenty-second Street and The Strand. *Courtesy Rosenberg Library, Galveston.*

year in which they listed furniture as personal property, a fact which suggests that in 1874 they began to acquire furniture which they perceived as being valuable. Two pieces of furniture from this period have remained in the Brown family and have been returned to the house. One is a Renaissance Revival armchair, with its angular crest, somewhat classical in inspiration, and its turned legs. Originally this may have been part of a suite of furniture used in one of the parlors, only to be relegated to the upper hall at a later date. The other is the sideboard at the east end of the dining room, in the Eastlake style. Again, it is likely that the Browns purchased an entire dining-room suite in this style. Clearly, their purchases of the mid-1870s indicate a desire to have their house furnished in the most up-to-date style.[8]

The valuation of Ashton Villa itself took a dramatic increase in 1877, suggesting that significant work was done on the house. The most important change was the enclosure of the space between the main house and the kitchen block to create the family room. This was an informal living room and dining hall, a soaring space with a skylight and a staircase curving down from the second floor. At the east end of the room was a wood and glass conservatory. The bricks of the north wall of the house and the south wall of the kitchen were painted white. The overmantel in the dining room was stained to resemble walnut and remodeled to match the Eastlake dining-room suite. For the family room the Browns purchased another dining-room suite in the Renaissance Revival style. The seats and backs of

The J. M. Brown Residence, Ashton Villa. Photograph taken after 1877. *Courtesy Rosenberg Library, Galveston.* This view from the southeast shows the exterior of the family room, which connected the kitchen block with the main house.

The family room, Ashton Villa. Photograph taken after 1877. *Courtesy Rosenberg Library, Galveston.* The huge windows of the cats' parlor is at the left, and the great fireplace is in shadow at the right. In between are overstuffed chairs, a hall stand with mirror, paintings on the walls, presumably by Miss Bettie, and a rather lethal looking chandelier.

these chairs were upholstered in leather. Finally, Renaissance Revival valances were placed over the windows in all the first-floor rooms.[9]

A historic photograph of the hall taken sometime after the creation of the family room shows that the Browns owned a large hall stand. This was a piece of furniture unique to the Victorian era, consisting of a bench, a large mirror, turned wooden pegs for hanging coats and hats, and a receptacle for umbrellas. The mirror was an indication of the Victorian preoccupation with fashionable attire and personal appearance, as were the pegs for coats and hats. Near the hall stand could be found another object especially popular in the Victorian era: a card basket. In the latter half of the nineteenth century ladies of the middle and upper classes called upon one another, and if they found no one at home they would leave a card in such a basket. Entire books were written about the proper etiquette of such calls, an indication of how seriously these visits were taken in the Victorian era.[10]

As is befitting one of the wealthiest families in Texas, the Browns ate extremely well. As they sat in their stylish Renaissance Revival chairs, they frequently dined on inch-thick portions of the most tender (and most expensive) cuts of steak: sirloin, porterhouse, and T-bone. They also were fond of turkey, chicken, pork, mutton, crab, and fish. Accompanying such meals were beer, ale, wine, or champagne. The Browns had their meals served on fine European porcelain, acquired perhaps through Joseph Sauter's furniture store in Galveston or perhaps by the Brown children on one of their sojourns in Europe.[11]

Dinner in the family room, 1889. *Courtesy Rosenberg Library, Galveston.* In the foreground Reba Brown, daughter of John and Helen Brown, looks at her fiancé J. T. McClanahan; in the background from the left are Mrs. Rebecca Brown, John and Helen Brown and their other children, Miss Bettie (raising a toast), J. M. Brown, Thomas Sweeney, and Mathilda Brown Sweeney. The Browns are seated in Renaissance Revival chairs acquired in the mid-1870s. In the background the back stairway cuts across the white painted brick wall, which was the original rear wall of the house.

The hall, Ashton Villa. Photograph taken after 1877. *Courtesy Rosenberg Library, Galveston.* A hall stand dominates the left wall, balanced on the right by one of Miss Bettie's large paintings. Several carpets cover the floor and the stair. The great hearth of the family room is visible through the rear door.

In the 1870s and 1880s James and Rebecca Brown entertained Galveston society lavishly at Ashton Villa. An especially important day on the Brown's social calendar was New Year's Day. S. B. Southwick recalled that "on New Year's Day most of the houses were open to callers" and that at the Brown residence callers "found everything as beautiful, lovely and entertaining as they could wish. Those who called were expected to attend her magnificent ball that night."[12]

The Brown's second son, Moreau Roberts Brown, studied medicine in Philadelphia and Louisville, receiving his medical degree from the University of Louisville in 1876. He then returned to Galveston, where he served as physician of Galveston County from 1876 to 1879 and quarantine officer of Galveston from 1879 to 1881. From 1881 to 1883 he studied at the schools and hospitals of Gottingen and Munich, Germany, and Vienna, Austria, specializing in diseases of the nose and throat. He returned to Galveston in 1883, but after eight years he accepted the position of professor of laryngology and rhinology at the Chicago Polyclinic and the College of Physicians and Surgeons of Chicago.[13]

The other Brown children soon followed the example of their brothers John and Moreau and went to study in Europe. Bettie, the eldest daughter, was in Vienna from 1881 to 1883, studying painting. Charles attended Racine College in Wisconsin, then became an apprentice watchmaker in Philadelphia. He lived in Europe at the same time as his brother Moreau, studying stone engraving and cameo cutting. In spite of Charles's artistic training, when he returned to Galveston he entered the hardware business with J. S. Brown & Company. After three years he quit, pleading poor health, and went to California. He worked as a seaman, as a rancher in West Texas, and in the hardware business in San Angelo. By 1892, however, he was back in Galveston and had entered the insurance business, at which he worked for twenty-four years until the end of his life.[14]

James M. Brown also took an active role in the life of Trinity Episcopal Church, serving on the vestry in 1864 and 1865. John S. Brown, like his parents, was a parishioner of Trinity, and during his stay in Europe he had traveled with the Reverend Benjamin Eaton. In 1881 John S. Brown was appointed to the vestry of Trinity, and he remained a member for twenty-seven years. From 1884 to 1900 and again from 1902 to 1907 he served as senior warden.[15]

John, in fact, became deeply involved in the planning of repairs for Trinity Church. At the April 22, 1881, vestry meeting the Reverend Mr. Bird appointed Henry Rosenberg, George E. Mann, and John S. Brown to a building committee to oversee the repairs, which were to the designs of architect W. H. Tyndall. However, one year later the chapel was not ready for use, and Henry Rosenberg resigned as chairman of the building committee. James M. Brown was appointed in his place, even though he was not a member of the vestry. Thus father and son worked side by side in overseeing the repairs to the church.[16]

The repairs were essentially complete by September of 1882, when the Galveston *Daily News* noted the "remarkable improvement" which had been achieved. "Before, where the interior finish was low and ungraceful, it is now high and vaulted. . . . The huge columns which formerly were very ugly and always obtrusive are now reduced. . . . The native colors of wood give to the whole a solidity, solemnity and beauty suitable to the holy place." At their next meeting the vestry approved a resolution thanking J. M. Brown for "his successful services in placing the interior of Trinity Church in its present beautiful repair."[17]

In the early 1880s the youngest of the Brown children, Mathilda Ella, was becoming a young woman and beginning to fully participate in the swirl of social life in Victorian Galveston. From February to June of 1883 the seventeen-year-old Mathilda kept a diary marked "Private—Hands Off," which provides a remarkable window into her life.[18]

Mathilda's life at Ashton Villa was a very leisurely one: her days and evenings at home were filled with sewing doll dresses, practicing the piano, writing letters to her brothers and sisters in Europe, or talking "through the telephone" with friends. She attended church with her parents every Sunday and helped to decorate the church for Easter Sunday. She went to Forbes's ice cream parlor with friends or to Dr. Carruthers to have a tooth filled. She went shopping with her mother and took buggy rides "down the island"— to the unoccupied, western part of the island—with her father.

An important part of family social life was "calling," brief social visits to the homes of friends or acquaintances. A family either "made calls" or were "at home" to receive callers. Mathilda's entry for Monday, February 26, reads: "Went out calling all day. . . Made 18 calls—tired out. " She apparently was not *too* tired because she made 12 calls the next day! For closer friends an extended stay was appropriate, and became an occasion for tea. In the evenings Mathilda attended the theater, concerts, and dances. Many of these dances were at the dancing pavilion of Garten Verein, a social club founded in 1876 by the German Americans of Galveston. Another was at the residence of a Mrs. Armstrong, and Mathilda "did not get home until 2.30."

Not surprisingly, there are numerous references in Mathilda's diary to her friends, both ladies and gentlemen. She usually referred to the men by their last names: "Mr. Castleton," "Mr. Crane," "Mr. Sweeney. " Especially important was "Mr. Sweeney," that is, Thomas Sweeney, the son of an Irish stevedore who was rapidly rising in business and politics. Indeed, when Mathilda began her diary, Sweeney was a member of the city council and was running for mayor of Galveston. He was running not as a Democrat or as a Republican but as a businessman with a "progressive" record. During the campaign Sweeney had to defend himself from accusations that if elected he would surround himself "with a crowd of low Irish." He also had to defend his vote of the previous year to spend $1,000 of city money on the annual Mardi Gras celebration.[19]

Mathilda must have been pleased to find that so prominent a young man was courting her, and excited by the color and noise of the campaign. Her diary entry for Monday, March 5, under the rubric "Election Day," reported that "about 9 p. m. Mr. Sweeney came in. Oh, dear me! Fulton elected. How awful. " Sweeney garnered 2,299 votes to R. L. Fulton's 3,288. On Tuesday Mathilda was "miserable all day. Mr. S. left on 5. 30 A.M. train for Chicago, to be gone six weeks." Apparently Sweeney was considering a move to Chicago, a prospect which made Mathilda very uneasy. Wednesday was rainy all day, and she practiced the piano a little but "went to bed early. Dreamed about Mr. S. Restless night."[20]

Sweeney had returned by April 18, but Mathilda was having her doubts about the relationship. On May 9 she went with him to the Garten Verein. "A great many out there, had an awful, stupid time." Less than a week later Sweeney called at Ashton Villa just as the family was about to go to a performance of *Cinderella*, and much to Mathilda's consternation, her father invited him along! "I wished he hadn't," she wrote in her diary. *Cinderella* was "very good," but the house was "crowded" and "awfully warm."

Things came to a head on Saturday, May 26. "In the evening Mr. Sweeney called, alas for the last time, and oh how I wished he had never come. I could just go into a convent where I never would see another man. Such is life I suppose but it is awful. I believe after all one's school days are the happiest in this life. A year ago I thought home would be so happy, now it has become anything but that. I could cry all the time if it would do any good. This is the first time I have given vent to my feelings in my diary for fear someone would get hold of it, but I cannot confide in anyone and must write in my diary for comfort. Although I ought to tell Mama all, I cannot do so. How glad I am going away soon, I almost wish it was *forever*! but one is never satisfied I suppose. Oh why should I be the cause of making anyone's life unhappy. I am not worth saving . . . I am simply good for nothing." Evidently it was Mathilda who broke off the relationship. Her parents seem to have thought a cooling-off period was in order and sent her to the resort at Sour Lake in East Texas near Beaumont.

On Saturday, June 2 ,Mathilda and her brother John got up at a quarter of three in the morning and were at the train station by 4:00 A.M. The train didn't leave until 4:50, but it arrived in Houston at 8:00, and Mathilda and John had breakfast. Then they caught a very slow eastbound freight train, which didn't get in to the Sour Lake station until 3:30. A two-hour wagon ride brought them to the resort.

Sour Lake was perfectly round, about an acre in extent, and according to one visitor it "was constantly boiling and bubbling, caused by currents of gas escaping from the earth." Surrounding the lake were some twenty-five wells and springs, each of which had different minerals in them. Patrons of the resort would drink water from the wells prescribed for their malady. In addition, they would bathe in the lake. One visitor recalled in later years that "It was a delightful sensation to plunge into the buoyant water and feel the pressure of the gas causing the water to bubble." Patrons could also take mud baths, which were prescribed "for every ache and pain" and which the ladies applied "to clear their complexions."[21]

Apparently the Browns were quite familiar with Sour Lake before Mathilda's visit. "The pioneer hardware man of Galveston, the late J. M. Brown, had during the War Between the States, a fine and valuable Negro cook, who became blind. Dr. Marant Smith, the owner of the lake at that time, induced Mr. Brown to send the Negro over, which he did. After several months, he received no reports but did receive several offers to buy the slave. They drove over to Sour

Lake to investigate and found that the Negro cook had regained her eyesight. She was taken back to Galveston."[22]

John returned to Galveston the next day, but Mathilda stayed for nearly two weeks. Some days she took a "sour bath," other days a "mud bath. " She embroidered, wrote letters, played the piano for the other guests, and joined with them in card games. On June 16 Mathilda left Sour Lake for Houston. She did not return to Galveston but went on to another resort in Lampasas, northwest of Austin. Unfortunately, Mathilda's diary ends at this point, or, to be precise, the remaining pages were ripped out. Apparently her reservations about Sweeney were overcome—they were married at Trinity Church on May 7, 1884.

As a wedding present, J. M. Brown had a house built for Mathilda and her new husband at 2402 Avenue L, little more than two blocks from Ashton Villa. The story-and-a-half wood-frame house is studiously symmetrical, but has delightful Victorian trim on the dormer windows and the front porch. The balustrade of the front porch consists of a series of wheels fashioned after the helm of a ship, striking a whimsical, nautical note. Including the land on which it was built, the house was a $4,000 wedding gift.[23]

By 1890 the population of Galveston had grown to 29,000, and by 1900 it would reach nearly 38,000. Broadway was still an unpaved street, but it was lined with great Victorian mansions. At Broadway and 14th Street architect Nicholas Clayton designed an extraordinary High Victorian fantasy for Colonel Walter Gresham. Said to have cost more than a quarter of a million dollars, the house is now known as the Bishop's Palace. And just one block west of Ashton Villa, George and Magnolia Sealy were building a grand new mansion to the designs of Stanford White, a principal in the prestigious New York firm of McKim, Mead & White. The Sealy House, with its sandy-colored Roman brick and red tile roof, was an informal Victorian version of a Renaissance palazzo. The interior spaces were in a variety styles, but one was especially significant for the later evolution of Ashton Villa: a Louis XVI drawing room with damask-covered walls and white woodwork with gold trim, known around town as the Gold Room.[24]

Thirty years had passed since J. M. Brown had built Ashton Villa, and the house had been planned on such a large scale and with such

The Gold Room, Ashton Villa. Photograph taken after the remodelling of the early 1890s. *Courtesy Rosenberg Library, Galveston.*

lovely ornamentation that it could hold its own against its newer Victorian neighbors. However, for someone like Miss Bettie, who had toured Europe and danced in royal castles, the Gold Room in the Sealy House must have made the Browns' 1850s French Antique parlor set look excruciatingly provincial.

Around 1890 Miss Bettie set about improving the large parlor. The French Antique sofa and four chairs were painted white with gold highlighting, and reupholstered in imitation of an Aubusson carpet. This set she placed in the center of the inside wall, opposite the fireplace. The mantel received a similar treatment in white and gold, and a large new gilded mirror was placed above this. Even a stray Gothic Revival chair of the 1850s was rounded up and given a new coat of white and gold paint. The 1870s Renaissance Revival valances were taken down and put into storage, and new gilded valances were installed. Miss Bettie's oil-on-corduroy paintings of "Two Cupids" were hung on the wall. The remodeled room was called the

Gold Room, a rather frank admission that the Browns saw themselves as being in competition with the Sealys.[25]

Also in the 1890s the spaces adjoining the family rooms were expanded. The conservatory was enlarged by a wood-framed addition to the east with rounded arches and pilasters, painted white. On the west side of the family room another small sitting room was added. This sunny space became a favorite haunt of the family cats and became known as "the cats' parlor." Also the east end of the stable was expanded to the south, creating its present L-shaped configuration.[26]

In 1894 J. M. Brown's health began to fail, and his doctors diagnosed his illness as cancer. In February 1895 he took a trip with Bettie and Moreau, "hoping to stay the disease," but he returned to Galveston no better and was confined to the villa. He died on Christmas Day, 1895, at the age of seventy-four. According to his obituary, "He passed away peacefully, surrounded by members of his immediate family." His funeral service was held the next day at

The Brown family in the Gold Room. Photograph taken in the early 1890s. *Courtesy Rosenberg Library, Galveston.* From left to right: Helen Delespine Brown, Mathilda Brown Sweeney, John Stoddart Brown and infant, James M. Brown, Rebecca Brown, Sarah Stoddart Rhodes, and Charles K. Rhodes.

Trinity, the church he had attended for nearly fifty years. The pall-bearers included such well-known Texans as George Sealy, J. H. Hutchings, W. L. Moody, and William Marsh Rice. The body was then escorted to the Episcopal Cemetery by the Knights Templar, an organization of which Brown had been the oldest living member.[27]

The Galveston *Daily News* wrote that Galveston had "lost one of her most successful and influential businessmen and Texas one of her most enterprising citizens. Scarcely an enterprise of importance has been inaugurated in Galveston during the last thirty-odd years that has not been assisted to success through the splendid business judgment and executive ability of Colonel Brown. " In addition to his business acumen and public-spiritedness, Brown was praised as being warmhearted, charitable, and devoted to his family. Such tributes, however heartfelt, are recorded on paper, which can become brittle and turn to dust. But J. M. Brown had built for himself a more solid and enduring memorial to his life and times: the house he called Ashton Villa.[28]

4.
TIMES OF CHANGE
AT THE VILLA

AFTER THE DEATH OF J. M. BROWN, the household at Ashton Villa consisted of Rebecca Brown, her mother Mrs. Rhodes, and Miss Bettie. Soon they were joined by Mathilda and her three children, Alice, Moreau, and Charles James. Mathilda Sweeney had filed for divorce from Tom Sweeney after thirteen years of marriage. Although she retained ownership of their house on Avenue L, he continued to live there until his death in 1905.

With a young family living in the house again, the Brown women decided to undertake another expansion of the house. The dining room and the northeast bedroom were extended to the east. The eastern end of these rooms had angled corners, creating a semi-octagonal bay. In the dining room a round-headed stained-glass window was installed in the end wall, and the Eastlake sideboard was placed just beneath it. The dining room now had one additional door and two additional windows; Renaissance Revival valances, perhaps those which used to grace the Gold Room, were installed. The enlarged bedroom above the dining room was occupied by Mathilda and her daughter Alice.

On the exterior the addition disrupted the original symmetry of the villa, but perhaps these changes made the house blend better with the numerous asymmetrical Victorian mansions on Broadway. The wood-frame conservatory east of the family room was removed, but its walls were used on the third floor as a partition between the old northeast room and the new addition. The eastern side of the third floor Miss Bettie used as her painting studio. This expansion of

The dining room, Ashton Villa. Photograph taken after the expansion of the house in 1900. *Courtesy Rosenberg Library, Galveston.*

the house began in the latter half of 1899 and was completed before September 1900.

No sooner had these changes been completed than Galveston was struck by the great hurricane of September 8, 1900. This tremendous storm killed some 6,000 people on Galveston Island and perhaps another 6,000 on the mainland. Practically the entire island was flooded, the high-water mark being 15.7 feet above sea level. At Ashton Villa, which is situated on one of the highest points on the island, the first floor was flooded to the height of 6 feet, forcing the women and children to the upper two floors, along with all the furniture and other valuables they could carry. Others sought refuge from the storm at Ashton Villa and the other great houses along Broadway.[1]

The wind and water did not cause the worst of the damage, however. The remnants of wood-frame houses and other debris formed a gigantic battering ram which decimated many other houses. Anything within six blocks of the beach from the eastern tip of the island to 35th Street was totally destroyed. After the storm a huge breakwater of debris anywhere from four to ten feet deep stretched for thirty blocks. Most of the buildings on the northern side of the island survived intact, but many hundreds of buildings, including Nicholas Clayton's Sacred Heart Church, across the street from the Gresham House, were totally destroyed. Ashton Villa survived the storm, but the winds did serious damage to the roof and uprooted most of the trees in the yard. In the aftermath of the hurricane, Galvestonians decided to build a great sea wall and raise the grade of the island to protect the city from future storms. Ashton Villa was not raised, but its basement was filled in, and the grade was raised some twelve to eighteen inches.[2]

The expansion of the villa seems to have been an expression of optimism on the part of the Brown women, but the years of the early twentieth century were ones of retrospection and of partings. Mrs. Rhodes died in July 1903; Dr. Moreau Roberts Brown died in Chicago in March of 1904 at age the age of fifty-four; and Rebecca Ashton Brown, the wife of J. M. Brown, died on October 14, 1907. Ashton Villa then went to Miss Bettie. It soon became evident that the family fortune was dwindling rapidly. In 1909 the J. S. Brown Hardware Company was forced to file for bankruptcy. These financial difficulties caused a rift between John Stoddart Brown and his sisters Bettie and Mathilda. When John died three years later at the age of sixty-three, neither Bettie nor Mathilda attended his funeral. Another tragic note sounded on November 10, 1916, when Charles, the youngest of James M. Brown's sons, put a gun to his head and pulled the trigger.[3]

Miss Bettie's activities between 1900 and 1920 seem to have been profoundly affected by the suffering she witnessed during the 1900 hurricane. In 1901 she took on the presidency of the lady board of managers of the Letitia Rosenberg Home for Women, a position which she held for seventeen years, until declining health forced her to step down. She was also on the board of the Lasker Home for Homeless Children. In 1914 Miss Bettie astonished her friends and family by converting to Roman Catholicism at the age of fifty-nine.[4]

In the teens social life at the villa centered around Mathilda Alice Sweeney, the only daughter of Thomas and Mathilda Brown Sweeney. Alice made her formal debut in 1909 at age nineteen, and two years later she helped celebrate the debut of her cousin Rebekah, daughter of Dr. Moreau Brown. Many social events were held at the villa, and in 1916 Alice married Henry J. Jumonville, an attorney from New Orleans, in the Gold Room. The couple settled in New Orleans, leaving Miss Bettie and her sister Mathilda alone at the villa.

Miss Bettie died on September 12, 1920, after an extended illness. Her funeral service was held at St. Mary's Catholic Cathedral, but she was buried in the Episcopal Cemetery alongside the other members of her family. This left Mathilda as the last surviving child of James and Rebecca Brown. Clearly the villa, built for a young and growing family, was too large a responsibility for Mathilda, and she moved to New Orleans where she lived with Alice and Henry. When Mathilda died on January 17, 1926, it was clear that Ashton Villa could not stay in the Brown family. The next year the house was sold to the El Mina Shrine Temple, the fraternal organization known as the Shriners. On the exterior little seemed different about the house: a neon sign announcing that it was the El Mina Shrine Temple was the only notable change. Inside, the first-floor configuration remained unchanged, and on the second floor the only change was the removal of the partition wall between the two bedrooms on the east side of the house. Unfortunate in terms of later restoration was the Shriners'

Miss Bettie in one of her everyday dresses. *Courtesy Rosenberg Library, Galveston.*

Ashton Villa during the raising of the street grade after the Great Hurricane.
Courtesy Rosenberg Library, Galveston.

demolition of the Brown's two-story brick kitchen. The new owners drastically expanded the family room to the edge of the property, creating a large new ballroom. The only elements in the room remaining from the Browns' time were the curving stairway and the wood-carved mantelpiece.[5]

The Shriners adapted the small parlor to the right of the entry hall as the ladies' parlor, and the dining room beyond this became a lounge. The Gold Room was used as an office with several desks, filing cabinets, and other office equipment. Upstairs the two bedrooms on the west side of the house were used as sewing rooms by the Eastern Star Ladies, a sister group to the Shriners. Across the hall, the partition between the two east bedrooms was removed, creating a large ell-shaped billiard room. The third floor was thoroughly utilized as well. The western portion was given over to a band rehearsal room, the eastern part to a locker room, and the space in the 1899 addition became a music room.

Although the Shriners took reasonably good care of their new property, the very fact that one of the fine old homes of Galveston was no longer used as a residence was an indication that the neighborhood was changing. In the 1930s the Victorian home at the other end of the block was demolished and replaced by a service station and tire store. In 1940 a new Sears Roebuck & Company Department Store was built just across 23rd Street, and most of the rest of the block was paved over for a parking lot. Its use as the Shrine Temple probably saved Ashton Villa from destruction.[6]

As early as the 1930s Ashton Villa was recognized for its historic significance. One of the earliest nationwide studies of historic properties was the Historic American Buildings Survey, one of Franklin D. Roosevelt's New Deal programs. The U.S. Department of the Interior hired out-of-work architects to produce measured drawings of historic buildings across the country; these drawings are kept at the Library of Congress. In 1934 and 1936 Houston architects L. A. Glover, Edwin S. Metzler, Jr. , James I. Campbell, and Hermon Lloyd carefully measured Ashton Villa and made plans, elevations, sections (cut-away views), and drawings of windows, doors, stairs, and other details.[7]

In 1966 the house was prominently featured in a new book, *The Galveston That Was*, with photographs by Henri Cartier-Bresson and Ezra Stoller and a text by the Houston architect Howard Barnstone. *The Galveston That Was* brought to the attention of Galvestonians and indeed to a national audience the riches of Galveston's historical legacy, at a time when that legacy was threatened by the wrecking ball. Under President Lyndon B. Johnson the Department of the Interior created a new form of recognition, the National Register of Historic Places, which sought to identify a wide range of historic properties so that their preservation could be incorporated into long-range planning. Ashton Villa was among the earliest Texas buildings listed in the National Register, having been approved in 1969.[8]

By the late sixties the Shriners began to feel that they had outgrown Ashton Villa. They resolved to sell the house, which raised in the minds of many Galvestonians the specter of its demolition and replacement with a more "profitable" building. The Junior League of Galveston seriously considered attempting to purchase the house, but the consensus was that it was too big an undertaking for the organization.

At this point the Galveston Historical Foundation became involved. The GHF had its roots in the Galveston Historical Society of the 1870s, but it was chartered and incorporated in 1954, after the successful effort to save the 1839 Samuel May Williams House. Twelve years later, in 1966, the western portion of the Hendley Building on The Strand was saved from demolition, given to the GHF, and restored as the organization's headquarters. A grant from the U.S. Department of Housing and Urban Development, matched by the Moody Foundation, the Kempner Fund, and the GHF, made possible the purchase of Ashton Villa. On September 16, 1970, the Shriners sold the house for $125,000 to the City of Galveston, which then leased the house to the GHF for the sum of $10 per year.

The GHF appointed an Ashton Villa Committee early in 1971, and attention was turned to the selection of a restoration architect. The committee eventually selected Raiford Stripling of San Augustine, Texas, one of the pioneers of historic preservation in the state. Stripling had been involved with the National Park Service's reconstruction of Mission Espíritu Santo near Goliad, Texas from 1933 to 1941, and after World War II he was involved in the restoration of the French Legation in Austin as well as a number of houses in his native San Augustine in far East Texas.[9]

Research on Ashton Villa and the Brown family was conducted throughout most of 1971. Records at the Galveston County Courthouse and at the Rosenberg Library were searched, all living descendants of the Brown family were contacted for information, and Stripling investigated the physical evidence remaining in the house. In September 1971 an extraordinary find virtually walked through the door: the younger son of Alice Sweeney Jumonville donated his mother's collection of family photographs, which included family scenes as well as many views of the house, both exterior and interior. These photographs were invaluable not only for the restoration of the house but also for the development of a furnishings plan and of a philosophy of interpretation.

Work began on the exterior of the villa in February 1973. The brick exterior, which had been painted at some time, was thoroughly cleaned. Many of the bricks were turned around, exposing an original, unpainted surface, and the outer layer of brick was given new mortar. Some of the woodwork needed to be replaced: wooden trim, rotting boards, and two sets of the brackets under the eaves. Parts of the cast-iron front porch were missing, but from the remaining fabric

Ashton Villa in 1989. Courtesy The Galveston Historical Foundation.

replacement parts were cast. The windows, especially the great triple-hung sash windows on the first and second floors, were restored as closely to their original appearance as was possible. When three inches of concrete was removed from the original porch floor, red octagonal tiles were visible. Such tiles were no longer manufactured, so modern tiles were painstakingly cut to reproduce the pattern.[10]

The interior was in reasonably good shape considering its years of use. On the first floor most of the original plaster cornices, center medallions, and gas chandeliers remained, as did the pier mirrors in the Gold Room. A central air conditioning system was installed, providing climate control for the protection of the furniture and other artifacts as well as for the comfort of the visitor. The most significant change to the interior was the restoration of the partition wall and closets between the two bedrooms on the eastern side of the second floor.[11]

For the furnishing of the interior, the Ashton Villa Committee turned to David B. Warren, curator of the Bayou Bend Collection of Early American furniture and decorative arts of the Museum of Fine Arts in Houston. Warren proposed an interpretation which would demonstrate a family's "progression of taste" in the second half of the nineteenth century. The exterior, the Gold Room, and the master bedroom would represent the earliest days of the house, the dining room would represent the Victorian era, and the small parlor would represent the Edwardian era. The bedrooms of Mathilda Sweeney and Miss Bettie would reflect their individual tastes and lifestyles. In the later phases of the interior restoration, Ellen Beasley, formerly of the National Trust for Historic Preservation, and Peter Rippe, then director of the Harris County Heritage Society, assisted in the selection of historic fabrics for carpets and curtains.[12]

Considerable attention was paid to the historic landscaping of Ashton Villa. When the house was built, a number of oak trees had been planted around the periphery of the property, but most of these had been blown down by the Great Hurricane of 1900. Subsequently palm trees had been planted on the grounds. Although these trees were not part of the original landscaping scheme, the restoration committee believed it was unwise to uproot seventy-year-old palm trees to plant oak saplings, so the turn-of-the-century plantings were preserved. The walks around the house and the driveway were restored, and the ornate cast-iron fence was refurbished.[13]

The restoration was completed in July of 1974. On the evening of July 25 an open house was held for members of the Brown family, Galveston Historical Foundation members, the Ashton Villa Committee, the project workers and their families, financial contributors to the project, and local, state, and federal officials. Two days later, on Saturday, July 27, the house was officially opened to the public. The municipal band played, civic leaders made speeches, and people came to look. What they saw was an ornate Victorian house, filled with the artifacts of six decades of living. Not quite so evident were the dedication and determination of a host of people who made possible the restoration of the house to its appearance of the late nineteenth century. Through their efforts an important part of Galveston's past had been recovered.

NOTES

1. INTRODUCTION: *New Year's Day*

[1] The standard biographies of J. M. Brown are Charles W. Hayes, *History of the Island and the City of Galveston* (Cincinnati, 1879), pp. 918–919; the obituary in the Galveston *Daily News*, December 26, 1895; John Henry Brown, *Indian Wars and Pioneers of Texas* (Austin, ca. 1896), pp. 712–715, which relies almost entirely on the Galveston *Daily News*; and Dermot H. Hardy and Ingham S. Roberts, eds. , *Historical Review of South-East Texas, and The Founders, Leaders and Representative Men of Its Commerce, Industry and Civic Affairs* (Chicago, 1910), vol. 2, pp. 555–559. Charles Hayes states that Brown was "born in the county of Orange, in the State of New York," and that his parents moved to New York City when he was but a child. However, the *Daily News* gives his place of birth as the city of New York, which is repeated in Brown and in Hardy and Roberts. Hayes states that Brown was apprenticed to a brick mason at age twelve, while the *Daily News*, followed by Hardy and Roberts, relates the stories about Brown running away and working on the Erie Canal.

[2] The date of Brown's arrival in Galveston is uncertain. The biographical accounts say he arrived in 1842 or 1843, but a search of the deed records of Galveston County revealed no property purchased by Brown before December 1846; this was supported by the Galveston County tax rolls. By contrast, it can be proved that Brown's future partner, Henry H. Brower, was in Galveston by 1843, because he paid the poll tax in that year. Hayes, *History of . . . Galveston*, p. 918, states that "In 1845 [Brown] manufactured brick on Carpenter's bayou," which is in Harris County, but an examination of the tax rolls of Galveston and Harris County found no ownership by Brown of any property in 1845. Hayes further states that Brown manufactured the brick for the county jail, built in 1845, and for St. Mary's Cathedral, built in 1847 and 1848. However, Brown did not own any property in Galveston County until 1847, or even pay the poll tax. If Brown made the bricks for these buildings, he made them as someone else's employee. Both St. Mary's Cathedral and the jail were designed by Charles G. Bryant, an architect-builder from Maine. On Bryant, see James H. Mundy and Earle

G. Shettleworth, Jr. , *The Flight of the Grand Eagle: Charles G. Bryant, Maine Architect and Adventurer* (Augusta, Maine, 1977), chapter 7. Mundy and Shettleworth state that Bishop John Mary Odin "in 1845 acquired a gift of 500,000 bricks from Belgium, which had been shipped without charge from Antwerp." This assertion has the glow of romantic embellishment about it, but if it is true, Brown was not the supplier of bricks for St. Mary's Cathedral.

3 Sydnor and James to Brown and Brower, March 31, 1747, Galveston County Deed Records, vol. F, p. 389, and Henry H. Brower to James M. Brown, June 15, 1848, p. 571 . Brown's purchase of Sophia and Harriet can be found in George H. and Jane L. Delesdenier to J. M. Brown, November 23, 1847, vol. H, p. 302 . Brown and Brower purchased Austin from Francis Moore, Jr., and Jacob W. Cruger, editors of the Houston *Telegraph and Texas Register*. I could find no indication that Brown ever sold Austin—perhaps he ran away or died in Brown's service. For Lucy and her three children, see James M. Brown to Eliza J. Bourman, May 17, 1847, vol. H, p. 195.

4 W. A. Fayman and T. W. Reilly, *Fayman & Reilly's Galveston City Directory for 1875-6* (Galveston, 1875), listed all mayors and aldermen of Galveston up to 1875.

5 The only biography of Rebecca Ashton Brown, Annie Doom Pickerell's *Pioneer Women in Texas* (Austin: E. L. Steck, n. d.), pp. 274–276, is completely untrustworthy. Some concrete information on the Stoddarts has been compiled by Texas Burroughs Anderson, *Cognitive Structures, Status and Cultural Affiliation: The Archeology of Ashton Villa* (Ph. D. diss., Rice University, 1985), p. 236 and Figure 6. My account is based on Anderson's data and the U. S. Census of Galveston County for 1850, p. 34, dwelling 251, and the Galveston County tax rolls for 1845–1851.

6 The *Civilian and Galveston Gazette* of April 14, 1848, reported that the Reverend Mr. Eaton married the couple on the ninth. On Eaton and Trinity Church, see William Manning Morgan, *Trinity Protestant Episcopal Church, Galveston, Texas 1841–1953, A Memorial History* (Houston and Galveston, 1954), especially pp. 24–33.

7 Galveston County Deed Records, vol. F, p. 389, and vol. T, p. 136. The Galveston County tax records show the property valued at $1,000 for 1848 through 1854, at $1,500 for 1855 through 1857, at $1,800 for 1859, and at $2,500 for 1860.

8 Hayes, *History of . . . Galveston*, p. 918, dates the Brown & Kirkland partnership to 1850, and this date is supported by the biography of Kirkland in *History of Texas, Together with a Biographical History of the Cities of Houston and Galveston* (Chicago, 1895), pp. 304–305. See also the U.S. Census for 1850, Galveston County, household 91. The Kirklands had a tinsmith from Vermont, M. Bowers, living in their household, suggesting that Brown & Kirkland was engaged to some extent in the manufacture of hardware as well as its sale. On "Auntie" Kirkland, see "The Diary of Mathilda Ella Brown" (1883) transcribed by Judy D. Schiebel, on file at Ashton Villa, pp. 5, 6, 14, and 15.

9 The *Texas Almanac for 1857* has an advertisement for Brown & Kirkland, illustrating its new building and listing its wares. The agreement with Theodore and Gustavus Oppermann is in the Galveston County Deed Records, vol. L, p. 359.

10 Galveston County Deed Records, vol. L, p. 359; on the Hendley Building, see Howard Barnstone, *The Galveston That Was* (New York and Houston, 1966), pp. 29–36;

for the Pontalba buildings, see Leonard V. Huber and Samuel Wilson, Jr., *Baroness Pontalba's Buildings and the Remarkable Woman Who Built Them* (New Orleans, 1964), pp. 36–48.

[11] Galveston County Deed Records, vol. L, p. 430.

[12] Galveston *Civilian*, September 3, 1860; Joseph Stowe's biography is in Hayes, *History of . . . Galveston*, pp. 919–920.

[13] "Documentation for Ashton Villa Restoration" (ca. 1973), Rosenberg Library; "Miss Rebecca Brown Dies after Long Illness," Galveston *Daily News*, September 14, 1920.

[14] On Kirkland's death, see *History of Texas* (Chicago, 1985), p. 305; Galveston *Daily News*, December 26, 1895; Earl Wesley Fornell, *The Galveston Era: The Texas Crescent on the Eve of Secession* (Austin, 1961), p. 186; Galveston County Deed Records, vol. N, p. 562.

2. FROM NEW YORK TO GALVESTON

[1] Jacob DeCordova, *Texas: Her Resources and Her Public Men* (Philadelphia,1858; rpt. Waco, 1969), pp. 238–239.

[2] Samuel Sloan, *The Model Architect* (Philadelphia, 1852) has been reprinted as *Sloan's Victorian Buildings* (New York, 1980).

[3] Sloan, *The Model Architect*, vol. 1, p. 88.

[4] I have consulted the Wood & Perot catalogue at the library of the Henry Francis du Pont Wintherthur Museum. The title page reads Robert Wood & Co. , *Portfolio of Original Designs of Ornamental Ironwork of Every Description* (Philadelphia, n.d.) However, all of the plates are marked "Wood & Perot, Philadelphia." For the advertisements of Wood & Perot's Galveston agent, see *Civilian and Galveston Gazette*, June 15 and June 22, 1858; on cast-iron in Galveston and elsewhere in the United States, see Barnstone, *The Galveston That Was*, pp. 55–66; Sara and Michael Southworth, *Ornamental Ironwork: An Illustrated Guide to Its Design, History & Use in American Architecture* (Boston, 1978), pp. 38–39, 68–71; on the Biamenti House, now the Cornstalk Hotel (ca. 1855), and the Short-Favrot House (1859), see U. S. Department of the Interior, Technical Preservation Services Division, *Metals in America's Historic Buildings* (Washington, D.C. , 1980), Figure 89.

[5] Galveston *Daily News*, December 26, 1895; on the price of bricks from various locales, see *Civilian and Galveston Gazette*, August 11, 1847, and November 21, 1854. Page 3 of the latter issue has the advertisement of N. D. Labadie.

[6] Sloan's double parlors were each sixteen feet by sixteen feet, Brown's large parlor was nineteen feet by thirty-six feet; Sloan's office was fourteen feet by sixteen feet; Brown's sitting room was seventeen feet by nineteen feet; Sloan's dining room was sixteen feet by nineteen feet; and Brown's seventeen feet by nineteen feet. The dimensions of Ashton Villa were taken by the Historic American Buildings Survey in 1934; the drawings are reproduced in David G. DeLong, ed., *Historic American Buildings: Texas* (New York, 1979), vol. 2, pp. 53–63.

[7] Andrew Jackson Downing, *The Architecture of Country Houses* (New York, 1850)

illustrates second-floor plans with closets, water closets, and full bathrooms. See, for example, pp. 283, 288, 309. A gas fixture very similar to that in the Gold Room is illustrated in Plate 18 of Denys Peter Myers, *Gaslighting in America: A Guide for Historic Preservation* (Washington, D.C.: U.S. Department of the Interior, Heritage Conservation and Recreation Service, 1978). My thanks to Rick Lewis of the Texas Historical Commission for introducing me to this publication.

8 Galveston *Daily News*, December 26, 1895.

9 Ibid.; Downing, *The Architecture of Country Houses*, pp. 432–433. William Seale, in *The Tasteful Interlude: American Interiors Through the Camera's Eye, 1860–1917* (New York, 1975), p. 201, illustrates the Gold Room, which he dates to 1907, and notes that the parlor suite was French Antique of the 1850s.

10 DeCordova, *Texas: Her Resources and Her Public Men*, pp. 239–240.

11 Sloan, *The Model Architect*, vol. 1, pp. 12, 88.

12 On the cost of the Governor's Mansion and other houses built by Abnér Cook, see Kenneth Hafertepe, *Abner Cook: Master Builder on the Texas Frontier* (Austin: Texas State Historical Association, 1991), Appendix I.

13 Galveston County Deed Records, vol. T, p. 136.

3. Life at the Villa

1 "Although he followed his state into secession, he was always opposed to that movement." Hardy and Roberts, eds., *Historical Review of South-East Texas*, vol. 2, p. 556. Other prominent Texans opposed to secession included Governors Sam Houston and E. M. Pease. On Brown's wartime activities, see Galveston *Daily News*, December 26, 1895. On the secession referendum, see Fornell, *The Galveston Era*, p. 293. On Brown's honorary military title, see Hardy and Roberts, eds., *Historical Review of South-East Texas*, and Galveston *Daily News*, December 26, 1895.

2 On Charles Rhodes Brown, see Hardy and Roberts, eds., *Historical Review of South-East Texas*, p. 559; biographies of John Stoddart Brown are in Charles W. Hayes, *History of . . . Galveston*, p. 973, and Morgan, *Trinity Protestant Episcopal Church*, p. 272. Eaton's obituary in the Galveston *Daily News* of March 26, 1871, as quoted in Morgan, p. 61, mentions his trip to Europe during the war.

3 Galveston *Daily News*, June 21, 1865; Hardy and Roberts, eds., *Historical Review of South-East Texas*, vol. 2, p. 556; for "Uncle Aleck," see Galveston *Daily News*, December 26, 1895. In a press release dated May 29, 1980, the Galveston branch of the National Association for the Advancement of Colored People states that on June 19, 1865, U. S. general Gordon Granger read the Emancipation Proclamation to the blacks of Austin from the second-story balcony of Ashton Villa. I have found no documentation to support this claim. When the order was printed in the *Daily News*, it carried the heading "Headquarters, District of Texas, Galveston, Texas," and it seems very likely that the proclamation was issued from army headquarters in the Hendley Building on The Strand.

4 On John Lang, see the 1850 U. S. Census for Galveston County, household 160; on Brown & Lang, see *Galveston City Directory* (1868); Galveston County tax records, 1868–1875; and Hayes, *History of . . . Galveston*, pp. 918, 973.

[5] These statistics are drawn from Ralph A. Wooster, "Wealthy Texans, 1870," *Southwestern Historical Quarterly*, 74, no. 1 (July 1970): 33–35. Significantly, J. M. Brown was not even one of the 263 wealthiest Texans in 1860.

[6] Hayes, *History of . . . Galveston*, p. 918; Willard B. Robinson, *Texas Public Buildings of the Nineteenth Century* (Austin and London, 1974), p. 119; Morgan, *Trinity Protestant Episcopal Church*, p. 271, dates Brown's election as president of the bank.

[7] Galveston Historical Society, *Historic Galveston Homes* (Galveston, 1951), pp. 42–43; the Galveston County tax records indicate that Brown owned the property from 1872, when it was valued at $5,000, and improved it in 1875, when its value increased to $7,500; *Galveston City Directory* for 1877–1878 refers to the house as Live Oak Terrace.

[8] Galveston County tax records, 1874; the figure of $1,600 for household furniture appears again in 1875; after that it seems to be subsumed under the category of miscellaneous property. For examples of Eastlake and Renaissance Revival, see Oscar P. Fitzgerald, *Three Centuries of American Furniture: An Illustrated Survey of Furniture from Colonial Times to the Present Day* (Englewood Cliffs, N.J., 1982), pp. 227–261.

[9] In 1877 the valuation of the house jumped from $18,000 to $28,000. In 1878 the valuation dropped back to $25,000 and eventually returned to $18,000. Apparently the changes weren't all that visible from the outside, and J. M. Brown saw no reason to pay taxes on them. The Sanborn Insurance Map of 1889 shows the family room and the conservatory, but not the sitting room (sometimes called the "cats' parlor") on the west. This room was added by July 1899, when the next Sanborn map was issued. The description of the additions is based on historic photographs, my examination of the existing fabric of the building, and the recollections of Rebecca Brown Slack and Lydia Brown Hanna, daughters of Charles Rhodes Brown, preserved in the Ashton Villa Restoration file at the Rosenberg Library. The Renaissance Revival dining-room set in the family room is visible in a family photograph of 1889. A very similar Renaissance Revival dining-room suite was purchased circa 1869–1871 by another merchant, banker, and railroad entrepreneur who owned an Italianate house in Sacramento, California: Leland Stanford. See Seale, *The Tasteful Interlude*, pp. 46–51.

[10] See Kenneth L. Ames, "Meaning in Artifacts: Hall Furnishings in Victorian America," *Journal of Interdisciplinary History*, 9 (Summer 1978):19–46.

[11] Anderson, *Cognitive Structures, Status and Cultural Affiliation*, pp. 220–221; Anderson's results are summarized by Daniel E. Fox, *Traces of Texas History* (San Antonio, 1983), pp. 361–365.

[12] S. B. Southwick, *Galveston—Old and New* (Galveston, 1906), p. 8. I examined the copy at the Rosenberg Library.

[13] R. French Stone, *Biography of Eminent American Physicians and Surgeons* (Indianapolis, 1894), pp. 64–65.

[14] On Charles, see Hardy and Roberts, eds., *Historical Review of South-East Texas*, vol. 2, p. 559; on Miss Bettie, see Galveston *Daily News*, September 14, 1920. Suzanne Morris, *The Browns of Ashton Villa* (Galveston, 1980), states that several of Miss Bettie's paintings which hang in Ashton Villa were painted in Vienna in 1882; this would coincide with the residence of her brothers Moreau and Charles.

[15] Morgan, *Trinity Protestant Episcopal Church*, pp. 271–272.

[16] Ibid., pp. 82–83.

17 Ibid.

18 I have relied on the excellent transcription of the diary by Judy D. Schiebel, former director of Ashton Villa.

19 Galveston *Daily News*, March 4, 1883.

20 Ibid., March 6, 1883.

21 Jesse A. Ziegler, *Wave of the Gulf* (San Antonio, 1938), pp. 147–151.

22 Ibid., pp. 149–150. Ziegler further stated that "Mr. Brown told me this story shortly before his death."

23 Barnstone, *The Galveston That Was*, pp. 193, 202–203; Galveston County tax records, 1886. The Sweeney-Royston House has been attributed to Nicholas Clayton, but there is no documentary evidence to support this, and the form of the house has little relation to Clayton's documented work.

24 Barnstone, *The Galveston That Was*, pp. 156–193; Jane and Rebecca Pinckard, *Lest We Forget: The Open Gates, The George Sealy Residence, Galveston, Texas* (Houston, 1988), pp. 49–56.

25 Seale, *The Tasteful Interlude*, p. 201, seems to suggest that the Gold Room dates to the early 1900s, and that the room might reflect the influence of Edith Wharton and Ogden Codman, Jr., *The Decoration of Houses* (New York, 1897), but a family photograph taken in the Gold Room proves that the room was remodeled before J. M. Brown's death in 1895.

26 Sanborn Insurance Maps, Galveston, 1889, sheet 27, and 1899, sheet 39; historic photographs of the house in the Ashton Villa Collection, Rosenberg Library.

27 Galveston *Daily News*, December 26, 1895.

28 Ibid.

4. Times of Change at the Villa

1 David G. McComb, *Galveston: A History* (Austin and London, 1986), pp. 122–128.

2 Ibid. According to local lore, the land around Ashton Villa was raised three feet, but archeological research indicates that it was half of that or less. See Anderson, *Cognitive Structures, Status and Cultural Affiliation*, pp. 201–202.

3 Information from Rebecca Brown Slack, daughter of Charles Rhodes Brown, dated March 19, 1971, in the files of the Ashton Villa Restoration, Rosenberg Library; biography of J. S. Brown in Rhodes, *Trinity Protestant Episcopal Church*, p. 272; Morris, *The Browns of Ashton Villa*, Part Five; on Charles Rhodes Brown, see Hardy and Roberts, eds., *Historical Review of South-East Texas*, vol. 2, p. 559, and Morris, *The Browns of Ashton Villa*.

4 Galveston *Daily News*, September 14, 1920, p. 3.

5 The Shriners' changes are documented in the Historic American Buildings Survey drawings, done in 1934 and 1936. See DeLong, ed., *Historic American Buildings: Texas*, vol. 2, pp. 53–63. The HABS drawings also indicate the Shriners' room uses. Further information was provided by Inez Lasell in correspondence with the author, October 5, 1990.

6 Sanborn Insurance Map, Galveston, Texas (1947), sheet 44.

[7] DeLong, ed., *Historic American Buildings*, pp. 53–63.

[8] James Wright Steely et al., *A Catalog of Texas Properties in the National Register of Historic Places* (Austin,1984), p. 62.

[9] Michael McCullar, *Restoring Texas: Raiford Stripling's Life and Architecture* (College Station, 1985); Kenneth Hafertepe, *A History of the French Legation in Texas: Alphonse Dubois de Saligny and His House* (Austin, 1989), pp. 35–38.

[10] Corinne Potter, "H.U.D. Project No. One: The Restoration of Ashton Villa," Ashton Villa Restoration file, Rosenberg Library; McCullar, *Restoring Texas*, pp. 136–137.

[11] Potter, "H.U.D. Project No. One," and McCullar, *Restoring Texas*, pp. 136–137.

[12] Potter, "H.U.D. Project No. One."

[13] Ibid. The fountain on the east side of Ashton Villa had been removed some years before but was returned to the house in 1979.

ACKNOWLEDGMENTS

ALTHOUGH THIS BOOK is not a massive tome, the debts that a historian incurs in writing even the briefest book are large. The original inspiration for this book came from the Galveston Historical Foundation, one of the most successful preservation organizations in Texas. Betty Massey, executive director, and Barbara Lawrence, director of Ashton Villa, have been enthusiastic supporters of the project, and Olivia Meyer has been patient and helpful in working through the myriad details that must be resolved before a book can be published. In researching the book I benefited from conversations with members of the Ashton Villa staff, particularly Karen Tircuit and Randy Kirk.

Across Sealy Avenue at the Rosenberg Library, the Galveston and Texas History Center contains a wealth of information about Ashton Villa and Galveston: newspapers, city directories, census records, wonderful photographs, and, perhaps most importantly, the files of the Galveston Historical Foundation's restoration effort. Lisa Lambert, director of the GTHC, was most helpful in retrieving files and photographs for me. The staff of the county clerk's office at the Galveston County Courthouse was kindly tolerant of my prowling through their most ancient record books.

In Austin, Michael Green and the staff of the Texas State Archives and Ralph Elder and the staff of the Barker Texas History Center were especially helpful in digging up old newspapers and insurance maps.

Inez Lasell of Galveston, who worked extensively on the restoration of Ashton Villa, kindly shared her time with me to discuss the restoration. Stephen Fox of Houston was generous with his knowledge of the architectural history of Broadway and of Galveston. And Bill Flynt, architectural conservator at Historic Deerfield, kindly gave me a condensed lesson in architectural drafting so that I could trace the floor plan used in this book.

Special thanks must go as well to Ron Tyler and George Ward of the Texas State Historical Association. I am grateful that the TSHA has developed their Popular History Series, of which my book on the French Legation was the fourth and this one on Ashton Villa the fifth. Ron has provided fruitful advice over the years, and George has helped immeasurably in smoothing over the bumps and jolts on the road to publication.

Finally I must acknowledge the support that makes it all worthwhile: that of my wife, Kim Troutman Hafertepe. Thanks again, K.T.